The Secret World of Hildegard

by JONAH WINTER

illustrated by JEANETTE WINTER

Arthur A. Levine Books

AN IMPRINT OF SCHOLASTIC INC.

 undreds and hundreds of years ago in

a time known as the Middle Ages, men

ruled over the earth. And these men were very gray. And the

buildings they built were very gray. And all the towns were

very gray. And all the gray towns were run by mayors who

were men. Girls were not allowed to go to school, and most

girls could not read. They were taught to serve and obey all

the boys around them. They were taught to keep quiet and

to be very gray.

Now it came to pass, in these Middle Ages, in the

kingdom of Germany a very special girl was born. Her

name was Hildegard, and she had great power that was

hidden from view.

From the time of her birth, she had the power to see a whole

world invisible to other people. Before she could even talk,

she saw a world inside her head so bright it made her tremble.

But she knew not what it meant, for she was just a baby.

And lo, when Hildegard was only three years old, she

predicted the color of a calf that had not yet been born.

Her prediction came true. This alarmed her parents. "How

could you have known this?" they asked. "You're just a

little girl."

Hildegard explained about the world inside her head. "There are flames and stars," she said to her parents. But after saying this, Hildegard felt scared. What if her parents did not believe her? What if she got in trouble?

And so, scared and alone, Hildegard kept this secret world

all to herself, safely locked away inside her head. But alas,

this brought on great headaches, and the headaches some-

times lasted for days. Sometimes, her head hurt so badly,

she couldn't get out of bed.

And there was grayness
and silence and sorrow,
though a light shone brightly inside her.

In time, it was decided that Hildegard would be sent away.

Her parents knew of a holy woman who took in special girls

like Hildegard. Maybe she could help this sickly girl.

On the way, Hildegard cried and cried. Why was she being

sent away? Did her parents not love her? Was there some-

thing *wrong* with her? Why couldn't she just be *normal*?

She believed in God, but where was He now? Why wasn't

He answering her?

Out of the mist, there arose a great stone building. It

looked like a castle or a prison. It looked very cold and

very gray. It was where she was being taken—*a monastery*

half in ruins. . . .

Even so, inside it was beautiful. There were flowering

gardens.

There were candles.

She heard lovely, haunting melodies.

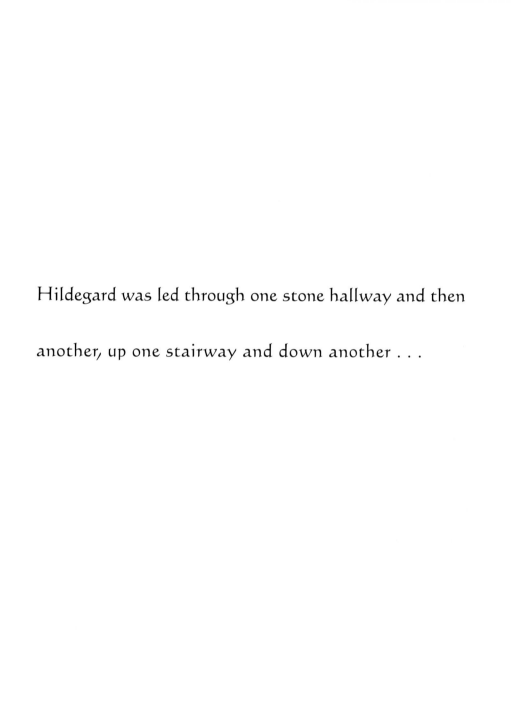

Hildegard was led through one stone hallway and then

another, up one stairway and down another . . .

. . . until she arrived at the big stone door of the room

where she was to live.

When she entered, she saw that the room was made entirely
of stone. There was hardly any furniture. And in the room sat
a quiet woman in a coarse black robe. "Welcome to your new
home," she said. And behind young Hildegard, the great stone
door slammed shut.

And there was grayness
and silence and sorrow,
though a light shone brightly inside her.

"My name is Jutta," said the solitary woman, "and I will teach you about the world."

And so, day by day, Jutta taught Hildegard many things. She taught her how to read. She taught her how to sing. She taught her all about the Bible. All day long, they studied and prayed, Jutta and Hildegard, safe inside their private world.

And it came to pass, after many years inside this room, that

Jutta died. And Hildegard, who was now a young woman,

decided to leave the room.

And Hildegard was such a good person — so wise and kind

— that the other women elected her "Mistress." As

Mistress, Hildegard was beloved of the other nuns and very

respected.

And yet, she was not happy. She longed to tell someone of

her secret, of the world she saw inside her head. The longer

she had kept this world a secret, the worse her headaches

had become.

And there was grayness
and silence and sorrow,
though a light shone brightly inside her.

Then one night as she writhed in pain, a voice spoke to her. And

the voice said: "This is the voice of God. And when you see a

great light inside you, that too is God. You must stop hiding my

light. You must let other people see what *you* see. You must let

the light inside you shine out."

Hildegard was terrified. So the secret she'd been keeping all

these years . . . was *God*? But what was she to do? She was

just a poor, little woman. And women were supposed to keep

quiet. Who was she to claim that God had spoken to her? No

one would believe her.

She would be laughed at, or sent away, or maybe even put

in prison. This world inside her head could get her in a lot

of trouble. And yet she knew now what it was, and she

knew who she was, and she knew why she had been put

on this earth.

And so, in fear and trembling, Hildegard began to tell her

visions to a monk and a nun, and they wrote her visions

down. She described the secret world inside her head, and

all that she saw there. . . .

And lo, she beheld the most beautiful flower hanging down from a flame surrounded by darkness, and a person as well was brought forth from the flame, and light from this flame began to brighten the darkness like the glow of a rosy dawn.

And lo, she beheld a woman of great size, as large as a city, all clad in gold and surrounded by angels, and she shone with the color of a purple hyacinth, and behind her stood a huge round tower whose windows were adorned with bright green emeralds, and this woman could not be destroyed in any way because of the strength of this tower.

And lo, she beheld the entire universe with all its stars, and in the center was the earth that was filled with greenness, and in the center of this greenness was a person who shone with the light of the entire universe. . . .

And these visions poured out of her, and she explained

what each one meant, so that others might understand her

God, who gave her all these images. And every time she

let her own light shine, the world was a little brighter, and

her headaches went away, and she felt as young and green

as a child.

And in time she had enough visions to fill an entire book.

It came to pass that her book was presented to the Pope, who

was in charge of all the churches of every kingdom. He would

decide if she, as a woman of God, had a right to be heard.

And lo, the mighty Pope approved of Hildegard and her divine visions. In no time at all, Hildegard was known throughout the land. People came from far away to behold this remarkable woman, to see if she was truly a prophet, to see if she was real.

What they found was a very real and very humble person, who took no pride in her great power. "I am just a poor, little woman," she always claimed. "I am just a feather on the breath of God."

And yet, the world looked on in wonder as this poor, little

woman blossomed like the Tree of Life itself. In time, the

tree of Hildegard bore so much fruit, the world could barely

contain it!

She wrote angelic songs that were sung by her nuns, who

dressed up in crowns and wings when they sang. Her music,

she said, came straight from God through her visions.

Everything she did came straight from her visions: a book

about medicine, a book about animals, even an alphabet and

an entire language.

In time, she became a great preacher and she preached across

the land. She preached that the force of God was strongest

in the small and poor and frail.

She wrote letters to her king, commanding him to change

his ways, abandon his pride. And the king wrote back to

her and paid her the respect that was her due.

And when she had finished her work on this earth, her secret world kept shining, because she had the courage to let it shine.

"In the year 1114 . . . a fiery light, flashing intensely, came from the open vault of heaven and poured through my whole brain. Like a flame that is hot without burning, it kindled all my heart and all my breast, just as the sun warms anything on which its rays fall. . . . Ever since I was a girl . . . in a wonderful way I had felt in myself (as I do even now) the strength and mystery of these secret and marvelous visions. . . . The visions which I saw I did not perceive in dreams nor when asleep nor in a delirium nor with the eyes or ears of the body. I received them when I was awake and looking around with a clear mind, with the inner eyes and ears, in open places according to the will of God."

— HILDEGARD VON BINGEN

Hildegard von Bingen was the most important woman of her time — and one of the most interesting people, male or female, of all time. That any one person could have accomplished all that she accomplished is astounding. That she accomplished these things as a woman, in an age when women had almost no power, is breathtaking. Although this book focuses on her development as a mystic visionary, she is now equally celebrated as a scientist — and most celebrated as a composer.

As a composer, she was the first writer of music whose biography is known. She wrote seventy-seven vocal works which were, at the time, revolutionary. Collectively, these songs are known as the *Symphony of the Harmony of Celestial Revelations*, and they are filled with the same imagination and powerful emotions that colored her mystical visions. In the last twenty years, her popularity has grown tremendously throughout the world as more and more recordings of her work have become available. The early music group Sequentia, in particular, recorded all of Hildegard's works just in time for her 900th birthday in 1998.

As a scientist, Hildegard's reputation has also continued to grow since her death. Her two scientific works, *Natural History* (about animals and plants) and *Causes and Cures* (about medicine), are still regarded as worthy of study. In particular, *Causes and Cures* now provides the basis for some alternative medicine in our modern world. In Germany, there are alternative medical institutes that practice the medical approach outlined in her book.

Within the world of the Catholic Church, Hildegard attained heights befitting a saint. There are those within the Church who refer to her as Saint Hildegard, though she was never officially canonized as a saint (mainly due to a medieval clerical error!). The date of her death, September 17th, is still an official Christian holiday.

But were it not for Hildegard's mystical visions (as recorded in her books, *Know the Ways of God, The Book of Life's Merits,* and *The Book of Divine Works*), and her courage to reveal them to the world, neither her musical nor scientific creations would have had the chance to blossom. For Hildegard von Bingen, all creativity was one and the same, and it all came from the same source, from God. Regardless of one's religious persuasion, one is tempted to believe this, since miraculously, this "feather on the breath of God" (as she referred to herself) was, by modern standards, uneducated. . . .

And 900 years after her birth, Hildegard still holds the power to affect the world around her, including the literary and artistic style of this modern illuminated manuscript, which was very much inspired by the visions of this incredible woman.

Bibliography

Bobko, Jane, ed. *Vision: The Life and Music of Hildegard von Bingen.* With text by Barbara Newman and commentary by Matthew Fox. New York: Penguin Studio Books, 1995.

Newman, Barbara. *Sister of Wisdom: St. Hildegard's Theology of the Feminine.* Berkeley: University of California Press, 1987.

Schipperges, Henrich. *Hildegard of Bingen: Healing and the Nature of the Cosmos.* Princeton: Markus Wiener Publishers, 1997.

von Bingen, Hildegard. *Mystical Writings.* Translated by Robert Carver. Edited by Fiona Bowie and Oliver Davies. New York: Crossroad, 1990.

For Dani~

Jonah Winter

THE PUBLISHER GRATEFULLY ACKNOWLEDGES PROFESSOR BARBARA NEWMAN AND
DR. MATHEW FOX FOR THEIR EXPERT ADVICE ON HILDEGARD'S LIFE AND TIMES.

LIBRARY OF CONGRESS CATALOGING-IN-PUBLICATION DATA

Winter, Jonah.
The secret world of Hildegard / by Jonah Winter; illustrated by Jeanette Winter. p. cm.
Includes bibliographical references.
ISBN-13: 978-0-439-50739-4 ISBN-10: 0-439-50739-1   1. Hildegard, Saint, 1098–1179—Juvenile literature.
I. Winter, Jeanette. II. Title. BX4700.H5W56 2007 282.092—dc22[B]   2006015990

10 9 8 7 6 5 4 3 2 1   07 08 09 10 11

The art was created using acrylic and pen on Arches watercolor paper.
The title type was set in CallifontsG68PostScript.
The text type was set in Calligraph421BT and CallifontsG68PostScript.
Book design by Marijka Kostiw

First edition, September 2007   Printed in Singapore   46